SUMMER

SUMMER

Ron Hirschi

Photographs by
Thomas D. Mangelsen

A WILDLIFE SEASONS BOOK

Cobblehill Books
Dutton • New York

Library of Congress Cataloging-in-Publication Data

Hirschi, Ron.
    Summer / Ron Hirschi ; photographs by Thomas D. Mangelsen.
        p.   cm.
    Summary: Baby animals spend the summer growing, playing, and
learning from their parents.
    ISBN 0-525-65054-7
    1. Animals—Juvenile literature.   2. Summer—Juvenile literature.
[1. Animals.   2. Summer.]   I. Mangelsen, Thomas D., ill.
II. Title.
QL49.H665   1991
591—dc20   90-19596
                                                                       CIP
                                                                       AC

Published in the United States by Cobblehill Books,
an affiliate of Dutton Children's Books,
a division of Penguin Books USA Inc.,
375 Hudson Street, New York, New York 10014

Designer: Charlotte Staub
Printed in Hong Kong   First edition
8 10 9

For Nuwhq'eeyt Kids
R.H.

For my brother Hal
and his children,
Eric and Kristen
T.M.

Run outside to play in the warm summer sun where the grass grows tall and sunflowers fill the fields.

Alaskan brown bears

Baby bears play just
like you.
They grow fat and round
on fresh summer grass
and learn to catch their
first fish dinner down
by the riverbank.

Summer is time to learn
and to grow.

Baby mountain sheep learn the safest path to summer meadows. Gosling wings grow stronger, their voices louder.

Canada geese

Dall sheep

Calliope hummingbird

Yellow warbler

Up in the trees, the songs of spring suddenly soften. Warbler mothers and warbler fathers, busy feeding their young, have little time to sing. Hummingbirds sip nectar for themselves and catch bugs for their tiny babies.

Baby birds flap their wings to beg for juicy spiders, beetles, and ants.

Mountain bluebird

Northern flicker

Then one day, the baby birds
finally fly, testing their wings
on the warm summer air.

Beneath the
cool umbrella
of forest leaves,
woodpeckers tap
for beetles.

Downy woodpecker

Nearby, bluebirds search
for diamond drops of dew
in the morning meadow.

In summer heat,
coyote's coat is
sleeker, cooler.

Coyote

Weasel sneaks
from rock to rock wearing a new
summer coat too.

Long-tailed weasel

And, ptarmigan hides
in feathers painted
like a summer
meadow.

Ptarmigan

Summer is time for
baby moose to grow,
and grow, and grow.
By summer's end
it is hard to tell
who is mother,
who is daughter.

Moose cow and calf

Moose

Now that his antlers
are fully grown,
the bull moose carries
a heavy weight.

Caribou grow new summer antlers too. They wander far to the north in the land of all night sun.

Caribou

Here at the edge
of polar ice,
great white bears
hunt in the longest
days of the year.

Snow geese

If you flew
with the snow
goose flocks
or with the
arctic loon,
this would be
your summer
home.

Snowy owl

The far north is where the snowy
owl hunts mice and lemmings, as
the long days end in summer's
last golden slumber.

Then, wolf howls ring in
the first crisp nights.
A cool wind feels like fall is
near.
Another winter will soon
be here.

Gray wolf

AFTERWORD

Summertime is a quiet season in many ways. Spring bird songs give way to soft chirps of babies begging while parent birds busily hunt insects or worms for themselves and their young ones.

Yet, summer is also a time of new sound, new growth. Baby animals learn the voices of the parents and others of their kind. They must also learn very quickly the sights and sounds of prey and potential danger.

Watch a flock of Canada geese as the goslings grow to adult size in one short season. Listen to their calls as the young birds finally catch that first gust of wind that carries them into the air. They are far more vocal now than before their wings were strong enough for this first flight. Capable of avoiding predators, do they laugh at a coyote's inability to chase them through the air?

Summer growth of most animals is incredibly rapid. Young elk must be strong enough for the demands of fall migration. Baby moose must have legs long enough to run from wolves when winter snow arrives. And, for many animals, severe weather at summer's end comes all too soon. In the far north and in the mountains, summer can turn to winter with no luxury of a lingering autumn. Hibernation or flight will help geese, loons, caribou, and other animals survive these abrupt changes in season. Rapid summer growth is a key to survival for the moose and others that don't move far from one season to the next.